Guess Who
Grabs

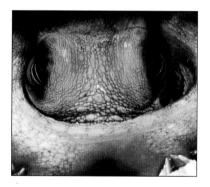

Sharon Gordon

BENCHMARK BOOKS
MARSHALL CAVENDISH
NEW YORK

My home is in the sea.

Come and see!

I live alone.

I am shy.

Here is my little cave.

I squeeze in and out.

It is easy without bones!

I am soft and floppy.

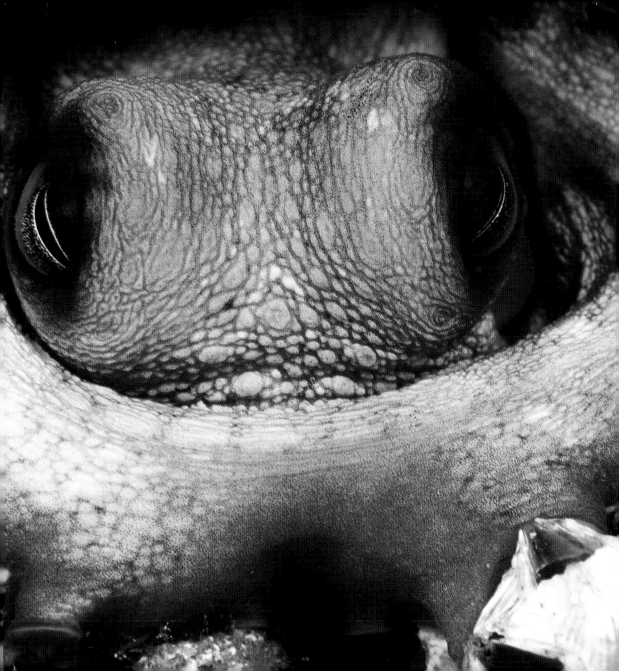

I have big eyes.

I see trouble!

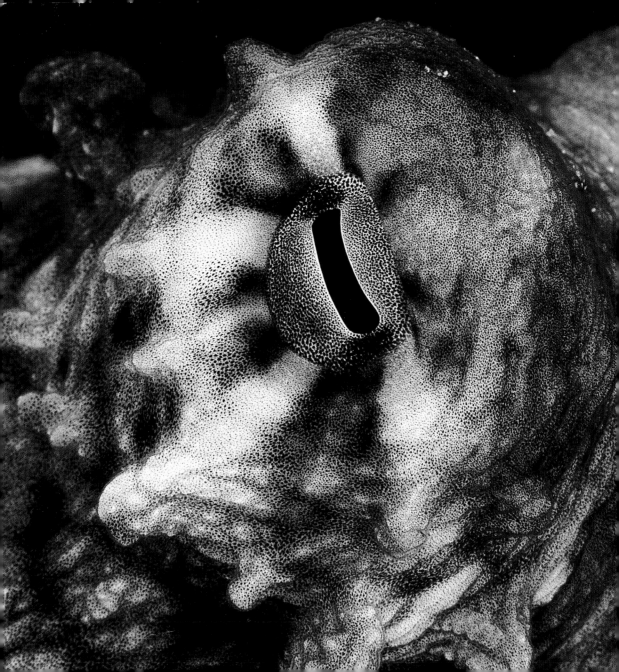

I can change colors.

That is how I hide.

I also shoot black ink.

It makes a dark cloud in the water.

No one sees me swim away.

I eat small fish.

Sometimes I chase them.

Sometimes I wait for them.

I grab them with my
long arms.

I have eight of them!

They are called *tentacles*.

They are covered with suckers.

Everything sticks.

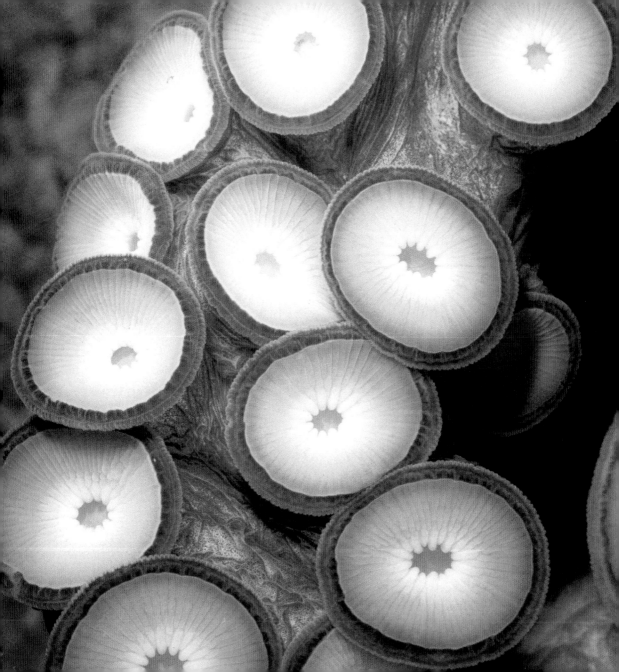

I lay many eggs.

My babies look like tiny fish.

Someday they will look like me.

Who am I?

I am an octopus!

Who am I?

eggs

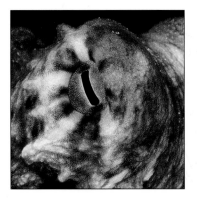

eye

ink

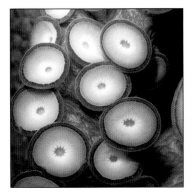

suckers   **tentacles**

Challenge Word

tentacles (ten-tuh-kuhls)
Long, thin body parts that an octopus
uses to catch food.

Index

Page numbers in **boldface** are illustrations.

About the Author

Sharon Gordon has written many books for young children. She has also worked as an editor. Sharon and her husband Bruce have three children, Douglas, Katie, and Laura, and one spoiled pooch, Samantha. They live in Midland Park, New Jersey.

With thanks to Nanci Vargus, Ed.D. and
Beth Walker Gambro, reading consultants

Benchmark Books
Marshall Cavendish
99 White Plains Road
Tarrytown, New York 10591-9001
www.marshallcavendish.com

Library of Congress Cataloging-in-Publication Data

Gordon, Sharon.
Guess who grabs / by Sharon Gordon.
p. cm. — (Bookworms: Guess who)
Includes index.
Summary: Clues about the octopus's physical characteristics, behavior,
and habitat lead the reader to guess what animal is being described.
ISBN 0-7614-1557-2
1. Octopodidae—Juvenile literature. [1. Octopus.] I. Title.
II. Series: Gordon, Sharon. Bookworms: Guess who.

QL430.3.O2G67 2003
594'.56—dc21
2003001663

Photo Research by Anne Burns Images

Cover Photo by: *Corbis*/Jeffrey L. Rotman

The photographs in this book are used with the permission and through the courtesy of: *Corbis*:
pp. 1, 9, 21, 29 (left) Stuart Westmorland; p. 7 Brandon D. Cole. *Peter Arnold*: p. 3 James L. Amos;
p. 5 Klaus Jost; pp. 11, 28 (top right) Kelvin Aitken. *Visuals Unlimited*: p. 13 Daniel W. Gotshall;
pp. 15, 19, 25, 27, 28 (lower), 29 (right) Dave B. Fleetham. *Norbert Wu*: pp. 17, 23, 28 (top left).

Series design by Becky Terhune

Printed in China
1 3 5 6 4 2